LITTLE LESSONS
in Faith

Text and Paintings by
KATHRYN ANDREWS FINCHER

HARVEST HOUSE™ PUBLISHERS

EUGENE, OREGON

Little Lessons in Faith

Copyright © 2003 Kathryn Andrews Fincher
Published by Harvest House Publishers
Eugene, Oregon 97402

Library of Congress Cataloging-in-Publication Data
Fincher, Kathryn Andrews.
Little lessons in faith: seeing God through the eyes of a child /
text and paintings by Kathryn Andrews Fincher.
    p. cm.
  ISBN 0-7369-0999-0 (alk. paper)
  1. Spirituality. 2. Christian children—Religious life.   I.
Title.
BV4509.5.F447 2003
242—dc21

2002010289

Design and production by Koechel Peterson & Associates, Inc., Minneapolis, Minnesota

Printed in Hong Kong

03 04 05 06 07 08 09 10 11 12 /NG/ 10 9 8 7 6 5 4 3 2 1

Contents

My Little Lesson in Faith   5

A Little Lesson in Faithfulness   6

A Little Lesson in Everyday Gifts   8

A Little Lesson in Talking to God   10

A Little Lesson in Hope   14

A Little Lesson in Trust   16

A Little Lesson in Unconditional Love   18

A Little Lesson in Strength and Courage   22

A Little Lesson in Friendship   24

A Little Lesson in Obedience   26

A Little Lesson in Paying Attention   30

A Little Lesson in Giving   32

A Little Lesson in Uniqueness   34

A Little Lesson in Tradition   38

A Little Lesson in Transformation   40

A Little Lesson in Promises   42

A Little Lesson in What Really Matters   46

Acknowledgments

To my husband, Jef, thank you for providing a loving stage…
so I can dance.

To the best two pieces of artwork ever…our beautiful daughters,
Maggie and Kelley. Thank you for gracing me as wonderful models.
Most of all, for being model children. You are the light of our lives.

To my mother for her love, encouragement, and continuous molding
of me as an artist.

To my mother- and father-in-law for guiding me through parenting
and loving me like their own.

To the parents of the beautiful children in my paintings. Thank you
for entrusting me with your children and sharing their "little lessons
in faith" with the rest of the world.

To the beautiful children in my paintings…for being children. As
adults we all need a dose of your innocence, wonder, and faith.

To Harvest House Publishers for believing in me.

Most importantly, thanks to my Heavenly Father, who enables me
to serve through His gift of art entrusted to me.

Faith

Show me your ways, O Lord,

teach me your paths;

guide me in your truth and teach me,

for you are God my Savior,

and my hope is in you all day long.

PSALM 25:4-5

When my husband, Jef, and I married, I was 33 and had no desire to have children. I was a nationally ranked trick water skier and an accomplished snow skier. To me, marriage was about sharing my love of sports with a life partner.

However, God has great wisdom and a sense of humor...I became pregnant in the first month of marriage! Motherly instincts did not kick in, though, and I was determined to remain unchanged by the pregnancy. I gave up the skiing but became obsessive about my tennis. In fact, I played my best competitive match ever, the state finals, during what turned out to be the initial stages of labor.

As I waited for Maggie's birth, I pleaded that God would change my heart toward children. "Please, Father, help me to like this baby as much as I love my dog!" And God was faithful. In one heartbeat, He transformed my fear and confusion into complete peace and understanding. I looked into the red face of my screaming baby girl and knew my first class on unconditional love was now in session.

God enables me to share my maternal passion for the spirit of our two daughters, and other children, through art. I emerge from my studio after painting or a photo shoot, amazed by a discovery. Now I share these insights, stories from other parents, and the little lessons in faith I have observed while painting these images of my daughters, neighbor children, friends, relatives—real children who are God's tiny teachers.

Let us begin our journey on the floor, eye to eye with the children among the pages of this book. Then, as we stand, stretch, and return to our adult perspective, let us better appreciate the special children God has placed in our lives.

Kathy

Faithfulness

Here's the church
Here's the steeple
Open the door
And see all the people.

Learning "Here's the church" was a very big deal to Mary Katherine. She practiced under the patient guidance of her friend Graham for a long time. When Mary Katherine's tiny fingers finally mastered the movements, she showed it to everyone!

Each Sunday Mary Katherine is so excited to get to church. She loves to sing songs and listen to Bible stories. She can't wait to share her new knowledge with her father and me, and now her little sister, too.

Our evening routine includes book time, teeth time, and prayer time. At just three years old, Mary Katherine says the Lord's Prayer as her part of the prayer, and then we close by asking God to watch over different family members or friends who are in need. Some have been on our prayer list for a long time, battling illness or financial hardship. While we worry about those who continue to face difficulties, Mary Katherine is always reminding us of the prayers that have been answered. She points us back to God's faithfulness daily.

~Loree, mother of Mary Katherine

*The greatest gift
parents can give a child
is their faith.*

KATHRYN ANDREWS FINCHER

*Here's the Church
Mary Katherine and Graham*

Everyday Gifts

Sam and Jacob are fresh from God and often share wisdom that has His imprint upon it. We know to watch for the gifts they reveal in the midst of our routines, schedules, and daily happenings.

Along the way, we have learned that fishing is important...and so is ice cream, laughter and snuggles, blanket tents and flashlights, stories and wild imaginations, baseball and baking cookies...everyday gifts from God, wrapped up in the small packages of our boys!

~ *Linette, mother of Sam and Jacob*

What do you call a fish that is large enough to keep? "A keeper." Children teach us to appreciate the simplest of "keepers" in our lives— family dinners together, washing the dog, roasting marshmallows, "balling up" white bread to use as bait. These everyday gifts are our catch and the keepers for our hearts.

KATHRYN ANDREWS FINCHER

"Come, follow me," Jesus said,
"and I will make you fishers of men."

MATTHEW 4:19

Keepers
Sam and Jacob

Talking to God

> *Now choose life, so that*
> *you and your children may live*
> *and that you may love the Lord*
> *your God, listen to his voice,*
> *and hold fast to him.*
>
> DEUTERONOMY 30:19-20

"Honey, tell Mrs. Fincher how God talks to you." The lady speaking looked behind her long skirt in search of her hiding four-year-old daughter. "Mrs. Fincher is an artist, dear, she paints skies and clouds—she will understand how God talks to you."

I was busy with a book signing, and it was not an appropriate time for a chat. However, the shy girl tossed her mother's dress aside as if it was a curtain and she had just been introduced on Broadway. The impatient line of customers mysteriously had extra time as she raised her eyes to the sky, stretched her arms up over her head, and opened her fingers as if someone Divine were about to pick her up.

"When the sun starts to go down, and the sky is pink..." she turned to make sure we caught step one, "that is almost the time. But when the clouds have red on the edge," she paused and emphasized, "*only* then...God talks to *me.*" She emphasized the "me" by placing both her hands on her heart. She held them there while searching my face—her fellow visionary as a painter of clouds.

Pick of the Bunch

"Can you hear what He says?" a lady asked as she bent down and gave up her place in line.

"Yes! But only when the clouds have red on just the edge." With that she dropped her hands to her side and reached back for her mother's skirt, knowing it would be there.

It was very clear to all of us that the spectacular sunset with the brilliant red-rimmed clouds this child saw was a private showing, exclusively crafted by God, so He could have a chat with a four-year-old.

Thanks to this little girl's message, sunsets have new meaning for me because…

when the sun catches the edges of the clouds,
and turns them into a brilliant red
only when they're a brilliant red…
God talks to ME!

And now these three remain: faith, hope and love. But the greatest of these is love.

1 CORINTHIANS 13:13

Thank you for the ones I love;

my father and my mother.

And thank you for my best friend

who is also my brother.

T.J. MILLS

*A Lesson in Grace
David and Katelynn*

A LITTLE LESSON IN...

Hope

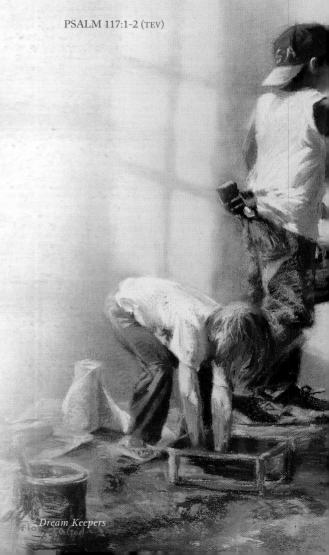

During the events of September 11, I had no desire to paint. I watched and I mourned with the rest of the world. But as an artist, creativity is my means of expression. And as a painter who expresses the life and gift of children, I could not remain silent.

As only God could orchestrate, I already had an overnight trip to New York scheduled. Once I arrived, I knew I needed to visit Ground Zero to fully understand what my painting should be about.

A gracious New York policeman arranged for me and a few friends to go inside the barricade. I expected to encounter chaos among the rubble. I was wrong. I witnessed a peaceful community working tirelessly with a sense of purpose. In the midst of the destruction were men and women, of all ethnic backgrounds, working side by side. There was a gentleness and kindness beyond measure.

Some say America's innocence is forever lost; we will never be the same. But I found a spirit of hope that was piled higher than any rubble. My painting reflects this hope in the children's unified creation of something beautiful while the shadow of a cross embraces their work.

My prayer is to pass along the lesson I took away from Ground Zero—this country can be rebuilt on a foundation of unity if we choose to embrace the promise of a future.

Dream Keepers

The promise is for you

and your children

and for all who are far off—

for all whom the Lord

our God will call.

ACTS 2:39

Trust

Katrine was afraid of the water and even more so of the "wildlife" that lived in its depths. Her older sister, Kristen, seeing how frightened she was, reached out her hand. Katrine's footprints in the sand faded away as she fully joined her sister in the surf—waves rushing around their ankles.

Holding tightly to the hand that guided her, Katrine knew she would be safe among the unnamed creatures of the sea.

~ Carla, mother of Katrine and Kristen

Just as the surf washes away
our tentative footprints in the sand,
our trust in the Lord will wash away our fears.

KATHRYN ANDREWS FINCHER

*For I am the L*ORD*,*

your God, who takes hold

of your right hand

and says to you,

Do not fear; I will help you.

ISAIAH 41:13

Unconditional Love

My nephew Dylan has an older brother Brit whom he adores. So when his parents told him that soon he too would be a "big brother" like Brit, he was so excited. And when baby Chad finally arrived, Dylan wanted to hold him all the time.

The newborn did nothing to receive Dylan's complete love, adoration, and protection. He simply came home and was swept up in the affectionate embrace of a big brother. When the boys' parents witness such pure devotion, they are reminded, "The best thing we have ever done for our children is to give them each other."

Dear friends, let us love one another,
for love comes from God.
Everyone who loves has been born
of God and knows God.

1 JOHN 4:7

Be devoted to one another in brotherly love.

ROMANS 12:10

The Homecoming
Chad and Dylan

Young hearts filled with hope

and innocence so grand~

Their endless faith and trust are held

in God's great loving hand.

T.J. MILLS

Perfect Fit
Ansley

See, I have engraved you
on the palms of my hands...

ISAIAH 49:16

Strength and Courage

*But those who hope in the Lord
will renew their strength.
They will soar on wings like eagles;
they will run and not grow weary,
they will walk and not be faint.*

ISAIAH 40:31

When the photograph that inspired this painting was taken, Austin was four and his brother, Brandon, had just turned one. We viewed it as a picture of an older brother talking to his younger brother. We did not know the image would take on a new meaning seven months later when Austin would be diagnosed with leukemia.

Austin was so strong throughout his three-and-a-half years of chemotherapy. There were times when we as parents thought that the load was too heavy. During his procedures, we would worry, cringe, and cry. Austin would comfort us by taking our hand and telling us not to cry—that it would be all right. And he never missed an opportunity to hug his younger brother.

He withstood many painful procedures and months of medication that would have broken the spirit of most adults. Yet his attitude and strength amazed many people and inspired those fighting battles in their own lives. He rarely complained. Even then, his complaints were more about the everyday things he missed—playing in the yard, going out to eat, going to school. In a world full of options, all he wanted was to be a kid.

*Heart Hugs
Brandon and Austin*

Austin has been in remission for two years now and lives life to the fullest. He remains an inspiration to us all. And we are sure that God has a special plan for our young model of strength. Kathy's painting has new meaning for us today. It is an older brother comforting his younger brother…assuring him that everything will be all right. It is a picture of our courageous son—letting *everyone* know "it will be all right."

~ *Jim, father of Austin and Brandon*

We are not at our best
when we are perched at the summit;
we are at our best climbing—
even when the way is steep.

ANONYMOUS

Friendship

A friend loves at all times.

PROVERBS 17:17

Bennett and Ashley were just three years old when this first kiss was shared between them. They are two firstborns with a penchant for ice cream, chasing seagulls, dancing, and each other.

Our families had met through the long and sometimes hysterical escapades of a Lamaze class, which bound us together. Then when our blond babies were born just 10 days apart in the same Atlanta hospital, a lifetime friendship began. It has survived career moves, relocations to other cities, family vacations, fortieth birthday parties, and all the triumphs and tragedies of school and sporting events.

This kiss of friendship took place during one of our mutual family vacations. At a Tastee Freeze in Florida, the kids ended up wearing more ice cream than they ate, but none of us seemed to mind—especially the kids.

Today, many years later, the Tastee Freeze is gone and these two blond babies are ready for college. Yet no matter how long they have been apart, every reunion seems like a time warp in which the past melts away, like the ice cream cones long ago, and these two enduring friends pick up where they left off.

~ *Kerry, father of Bennett*

A friend is someone who
reaches out for your hand…
and touches your heart.

KATHLEEN GROVE

Love Prints
Ashley and Bennett

A LITTLE LESSON IN...

Obedience

One day I looked out my kitchen window and saw a neighbor girl pushing her baby stroller down the hill. I stopped and did a double take when I noticed a strange, hairy leg hanging over the top of the stroller and a tail and two more legs falling through the opening beneath.

Oh, how this scene demonstrates how we express our love! Kate is the doting young mother, Betsy the dog is the cooperative child, and her friend is the loyal helper.

And although the determined, creative flair of a child was the catalyst for this image, it is easy to see that Betsy the dog is teaching the most important faith lesson—obedience.

Whoever has my commands
and obeys them,
he is the one who loves me.

JOHN 14:21

Things We Do for Love
Kate and Friends

HOME
TEAM

Lord keep safe the little ones

within my heart so dear.

Guide them with your loving strength

and always keep them near.

T.J. MILLS

Whoever trusts in the Lord is kept safe.

PROVERBS 29:25

Cooties
A Local Baseball Team

Paying Attention

When my daughters Maggie and Kelley were babies, Kelley came into my studio and told me to come upstairs right away. "Maggie needs you," she said with the grave seriousness a three-year-old can surprisingly convey.

I said, "Okay," but continued to paint.

Kelley walked over to my easel and said, "Mom, what's more important? That eye you're painting or your daughter?"

Sometimes children convict us with their questions. And while the girls often extended grace to me in the midst of one of my focused moments, Kelley knew she had a lesson to teach her mother. Her lesson for me that day on "paying attention" also included turning off my studio light!

Look with your eyes
and hear with your ears and pay attention
to everything I am going to show you,
for that is why you have been brought here.

EZEKIEL 40:4

*A little lesson
for parenting is to be
an attentive audience.*

KATHRYN ANDREWS FINCHER

*Social Graces
Maggie and Kelley*

Giving

Children wear their hearts on their faces. They challenge us with the narrowing of their eyes and the determined tightening of their mouth.

Such is the case of this young girl holding her beloved bunny. Notice how protective she is. She is hesitant to relax her grip on her cherished, furry friend. When people view this girl in the straw hat, they ask me...will she share the bunny? Or snatch it away?

Even as adults, it is easy to hold tightly to the things we love, forgetting about the tremendous joy of giving.

Would you share your bunny?

So let each one give
as he purposes in his heart,
not grudgingly or of necessity;
for God loves a cheerful giver.

2 CORINTHIANS 9:7-8 (NKJV)

 All Mine

For where your treasure is, there your heart will be also.

MATTHEW 6:21

Uniqueness

The differences among siblings can be surprising. Often we mothers and fathers reflect that it's hard to believe our children have the same parents. I sum up our daughters' differences by saying, "One eats the bread and the other the crust."

Such is the case for two young brothers as they prepare to play music. Four-year-old Michael sits on the bench and studies the sheets of music before approaching the piano keys. McNeill, on the other hand, is a child of action, preferring a direct approach. This captured moment in time sheds so much light on how these two boys relate to the world in their own unique ways.

When we observe children, their individuality unfolds. Created in the image of God, all children share something in common, yet no two are the same—just like sounds from piano keys. These many gifts and talents reflect the beautiful variety that God extends to all of His creation. We come in so many shapes, sizes, and styles. This uniqueness allows us to create life music to call our very own.

The woods would be silent
if no birds sang
except those who sang best.

HENRY VAN DYKE

For you created

my inmost being;

you knit me together

in my mother's womb.

I praise you because I am

fearfully and wonderfully made;

your works are wonderful,

I know that full well.

PSALM 139:13-14

Take Note
Michael and McNeill

Let us continually offer

to God a sacrifice of praise—

the fruit of lips that confess his name.

HEBREWS 13:15

Little Light, Be Mine
Kyle and Dusty

Good morning, good night

Good in between~

Thank the good Lord

For all that we've seen

———— ∞∞∞ ————

T.J. MILLS

A LITTLE LESSON IN...
Tradition

*Train a child
in the way he should go,
and when he is old
he will not turn from it.*

PROVERBS 22:6

On a wintry December day in 1948, my mother called me in from playing and told me to put on one of the lace-trimmed gowns she made for me. Our town photographer, historian, and postmaster took a picture of me as I said my prayers. My mother used it as her Christmas cards that year, and Kathy later painted it.

And though I posed for that picture, it really was the scene that could be found in our home every evening. We had a tradition of prayer that has always stayed with me. Every night before going to sleep, my father read the Bible and then knelt by his bed and said his prayers. Sometimes I prayed along with him. However, most often, my mother would lift me up so that I could kiss "the baby Jesus" on the Victorian mantel clock and go to my bedroom where I would kneel by my little iron bed and say my prayers. My mother always listened to my prayers, tucked me into bed, and wrapped my feet in a blanket warmed by the fire.

~Meredith, Kathryn's beloved cousin

Little Light of Mine
Meredith

*Give thanks to the L*ORD*, for he is good;*

his love endures forever.

PSALM 118:1

Transformation

See, I am doing a new thing!

Now it springs up;

do you not perceive it?

ISAIAH 43:19

My daughter Maggie, captivated by the beauty of a butterfly, is just seven years old in the photo that inspired this painting. "Chrysalis" is the story of a young girl on her spiritual journey, wishing to be like the monarch butterfly that has lit before her eyes. It is the story of a child's dream of her transformation.

Today Jef, the girls, and I are flying across the country to a family wedding on the West Coast. I look across the aisle at Maggie, now approaching sixteen. With fresh eyes I realize that Maggie isn't cute…she is beautiful! With her new dress on and her braces off, she is a young lady. When did she transform into a butterfly? Why had I not seen it?

I reflect over her past year in high school and realize Maggie is maturing in so many ways—spiritually, physically, emotionally, socially—she is becoming herself.

Recently she had to sit on a swim ring during her high school classes to ease the pain of a pole-vaulting injury. When I questioned her about kids making fun of her, Maggie's reply touched me. "Mom," she explained, "I know that I look silly with the swim ring. I can try to be cool and do things to make kids like me. But if I did," she added, "I wouldn't like myself."

I thank God for His perfect timing. As we fly to this family wedding, I realize I also have a daughter who has stretched her wings to fly…and she's more beautiful than any butterfly I can ever paint.

*And we, who with unveiled faces
all reflect the Lord's glory, are being
transformed into his likeness with
ever-increasing glory, which comes
from the Lord, who is the Spirit.*

2 CORINTHIANS 3:18

Chrysalis
Maggie

Promises

Alexandra *loves* animals. Especially kittens.

Unfortunately, I, her father, am allergic.

On any given visit to her grandmother Mema's house, you can find Alexandra playing pretend school. She carefully gathers her students—fifteen carved animals—and meticulously arranges them in a semi-circle. These animals are arranged by size and classification (water fowl, birds, bovine…yes, there is a Texas longhorn).

After getting everything just right, she begins her lesson. She sings to the carvings and shares her lessons from preschool that week. As you can imagine, the collecting and arranging process takes so long that just about the time she gets started with the schooling, it is time to start her clean up—a process throughout which she is still very focused.

Alexandra's favorite Bible verse is Genesis 9:16. We call it "God's promise of the rainbow," and it always reminds me of her commitment to her class of carved animals. I may not be able to promise my daughter a kitten, but I can promise to always care for her as she so attentively cares for her "students" and as God cares for all His creatures.

~ Donnie, father of Alexandra

Whenever the rainbow appears in the clouds, I will see it and remember the everlasting covenant between God and all living creatures of every kind on the earth.

GENESIS 9:16

May your unfailing love
come to me, O LORD,
your salvation according
to your promise.

PSALM 119:41

Finder's Keepers
Alexandra

God grant me the patience

to slow my harried pace.

To gaze on simple wonders through

a child's wide~eyed face.

—T.J. MILLS

Gonna Watch or Fish
David

David is an observer. Whether he is fishing,
playing, or visiting my studio, he carefully takes
in a situation before forming an opinion—
an opinion he will eagerly share. When this
clever middle-schooler ventures from his home
next door and joins me in my studio,
I know my best critic has arrived!
From color selection to possible marketing tactics,
David is not at a loss for ideas.

And the great part about it…
I have learned to really listen to the fresh,
wonderful observations and suggestions offered
by all children. Their insights not only shed
light on the moment—they often reveal
a God's-eye-view lesson on life.

A LITTLE LESSON IN...
What Really Matters

My son Mason is full of goodness and wonder. His thankful heart, patience, and selflessness are worthy of striving for every day. The one "something" that consistently amazes me is his ability to discern those things that truly matter—like stopping to give God's creatures the awe they deserve—from those things that don't. So many times I've looked to Mason to better understand how I should be living my life.

~ Gary, father of Mason

*God knelt down and kissed
the trees and they did blush,
bursting forth with color magnificent…
and all for the love of a child.*

MARY SLADE LAIL

Work Can Wait
Mason

A child's eyes! Those clear wells of undefiled thought!

What on earth can be more beautiful?

Full of hope, love, and curiosity, they meet your own.

In prayer, how earnest!

In joy, how sparkling!

In sympathy, how tender!

CAROLINE NORTON